STAYING ON TOP

A 31 Day Devotional
Plus 21 Day Fast Inspirations

ENTER INTO HIS GATES WITH THANKSGIVING!
ENTER INTO HIS COURTS WITH PRAISE!

Pastor Otis F. Brown Jr.

Copyright © 2012 Otis Brown

All rights reserved. No part of this book may be used or reproduced by any means, graphic, electronic, or mechanical, including photocopying, recording, taping or by any information storage retrieval system without the written permission of the publisher except in the case of brief quotations embodied in critical articles and reviews.

WestBow Press books may be ordered through booksellers or by contacting:

WestBow Press
A Division of Thomas Nelson
1663 Liberty Drive
Bloomington, IN 47403
www.westbowpress.com
1-(866) 928-1240

Because of the dynamic nature of the Internet, any web addresses or links contained in this book may have changed since publication and may no longer be valid. The views expressed in this work are solely those of the author and do not necessarily reflect the views of the publisher, and the publisher hereby disclaims any responsibility for them.

Any people depicted in stock imagery provided by Thinkstock are models, and such images are being used for illustrative purposes only.

Certain stock imagery © Thinkstock.

ISBN: 978-1-4497-5816-5 (sc)
ISBN: 978-1-4497-5849-3 (hc)
ISBN: 978-1-4497-5817-2 (e)

Library of Congress Control Number: 2012911629

Printed in the United States of America

WestBow Press rev. date: 07/12/2012

In honor and memory of
Drs. Otis and Johnnie Mae Brown

Contents

Preface ix
Introduction xi

Thirty-One-Day Devotional

Day 1—Get a Good Start 1
Day 2—One or the Other 3
Day 3—Just Like Pa 5
Day 4—Night and Day 7
Day 5—Staying in Place: In the Sea, not in a Pocket! 9
Day 6—Here Comes Man 11
Day 7—Almighty God, Creator of Everything 13
Day 8—Obedience at Any Cost 15
Day 9—The Nine: Not Fine 17
Day 10—With My Hands, I Will Praise You! 19
Day 11—And Then There Were Eleven 21
Day 12—Spending Quality Time with Jesus 23
Day 13—In the World, but Not of the World 25
Day 14—Loving on God 27
Day 15—Sometimes, It's Wall Time 29
Day 16—You Young Whippersnapper! 31
Day 17—When Bad Things Happen to Good People 33
Day 18—Straighten Up and Fly Right 35
Day 19—You Are the Declared Winner! 37
Day 20—Counting the Cost 39

Day 21—The Answer Is Coming 41
Day 22—Fear Not! 43
Day 23—Each Day Makes a Difference 45
Day 24—The Mind of Worship 47
Day 25—Just Do the Right Thing 49
Day 26—You Are Making a Difference 51
Day 27—Destined for Greatness 53
Day 28—The Gift of Singing 55
Day 29—The Gift from Mother 57
Day 30—Choose Life 59
Day 31—A Vessel of Honor 61

Twenty-One-Day Fast

Day 1 65
Day 2 67
Day 3 69
Day 4 71
Day 5 73
Day 6 75
Day 7 77
Day 8 79
Day 9 81
Day 10 83
Day 11 85
Day 12 87
Day 13 89
Day 14 91
Day 15 93
Day 16 95
Day 17 97
Day 18 99
Day 19 101
Day 20 103
Day 21 105

About the Author 107

Preface

I am who I am only because of the mercy and grace of God. Secondly, I am a product of two generations of deacons, preachers, and pastors who have preceded me.

Specifically, I am the product of my father and mother, who are now enjoying the presence of our Lord and Savior. They lived such an exemplary life before me and my siblings that we will forever bear the impact and influence of godly parents.

Never have I observed more the missing ingredient of godly parents or guardians than in our homes today. With everything that is within me, I say: *Thank you, Ma and Pa.*

Otis F. Brown Jr.

Introduction

This thirty-one-day devotional draws primarily on the inspiring Word of God. The author has sprinkled in short reflections of his growing up in Portland, Oregon, and Seattle, Washington, in order to demonstrate the practicality of everyday experience, both serious and comical. The insights and comparisons will surely resonate in your spirit. You will be blessed and eagerly look forward to the next day's devotion.

The twenty-one-day fast's inspirations have been written to help those who will dare to discipline themselves to hear God like never before. Our entire church does this every year, and it has proven to be a tremendous blessing for all involved and for the church as a whole. If we ever need to hear from God, it is now!

Day 1—Get a Good Start

Genesis 1:3–5 (KJV)
*And God said, Let there be light: and there was light. 4 And God saw the light, that it was good: and God divided the light from the darkness. 5 And God called the light Day, and the darkness he called Night. And the evening and the morning were the **first** day.*

Today is the first day of the rest of your life! You have the DNA of God formed, created, shaped, and breathed into your being. You are a living soul, created in the image of God. *You are holy dirt.*

You have been granted the power to speak light and life into your being, your family, fellow workmen, schoolmates, and brothers and sisters in your Christian family.

This is not a day you should make resolutions *to do*—instead, choose *to be* and *to become*. This will be a great day because you will speak it into being. God is waiting for assignments from you. Don't bore God with small thinking. Think big, ask big, and receive blessings both big and small.

Proactive **Q**uestions—

1. Who can I call and encourage today to look to the Creator of heaven and earth?

2. Is there a neighbor on my block that God is prompting me to introduce myself to?

>
> Psalm 118:24 (KJV)
> *This is the day which the Lord hath made;
> we will rejoice and be glad in it.*

Stay on top!

Day 2—One or the Other

GENESIS 1:6–8 (GW)
*Then God said, "Let there be a horizon in the middle of the water in order to separate the water." 7 So God made the horizon and separated the water above and below the horizon. And so it was. 8 God named what was above the horizon sky. There was evening, then morning a **second** day.*

God made a clear distinction between day and night on the first day, and now we see Him distinguish between the sky above and the water below. Relating to the Christian's position in the world, the Bible clearly informs us that we are in the world but not of the world. Jesus gave His life that we might show and live a clear and definitive difference.

Choose today to rejoice and accept God's sovereign will in your life. You just might convince those who are lost to surrender their lives to God.

To a caged eagle that has been finally freed, the sky looks mighty good. To a thirsty elephant that has traveled many miles with nothing to drink, water means sustaining life.

God left no fence to sit on. The Word of God burns up the proverbial fence that Satan would have us think exists. Let there be no confusion in the message of who you are today.

Proactive Questions—

1. Am I doing anything that might send the wrong signal to the people I want to come to know Christ as their Savior and Lord? Can I stop this behavior?
2. What can I do for those people today that will show them that I love them?

Psalm 19:14 (KJV)
Let the words of my mouth and the meditation of my heart be acceptable in thy sight, O Lord, my strength and my redeemer.

Stay on top!

Day 3—Just Like Pa

Genesis 1:12–13 (GW)
*The earth produced vegetation: plants bearing seeds, each according to its own type, and trees bearing fruit with seeds, each according to its own type. God saw that they were good. 13 There was evening, then morning—a **third** day.*

I am my father's son. I am also God's son.

It is so amazing how God set the sowing and fruit-bearing process in place. In fact, God did such a good job that He hasn't had to adjust it since He began the process.

Visiting my grandpa in Texas at about ten years old, he took us to the watermelon field and told me and my siblings we could all have a watermelon. We had to roll them to the wagon being towed by the farm tractor because they were so big and heavy.

Later, while smothering my face up to my ears in watermelon, I wondered how something so big could come from such a small, single black seed. The answer—God created it that way.

Choose today to reflect your Father God's characteristics and attributes.

Proactive Questions—

1. What can I do today that will plant a seed in someone's life?
2. Who can I spiritually water today to encourage the potential fruit I know is there?

1 CORINTHIANS 15:37–38 (GW)
What you plant, whether it's wheat or something else, is only a seed. It doesn't have the form that the plant will have. 38 God gives the plant the form he wants it to have. Each kind of seed grows into its own form.

Watching my father work as a pastor for fifty years has left an indelible impression on me. Without a doubt, I have some physical and spiritual traits of my natural and spiritual father. I am "just like Pa."

Stay on top!

Day 4—Night and Day

Genesis 1:16–19 (KJV)
*And God made two great lights; the greater light to rule the day, and the lesser light to rule the night: he made the stars also. 17 And God set them in the firmament of the heaven to give light upon the earth, 18 And to rule over the day and over the night, and to divide the light from the darkness: and God saw that it was good. 19 And the evening and the morning were the **fourth** day.*

When God set the day from the night, he also created the sun as the "greater light" for the daytime and the moon as the "lesser light" for the nighttime. At this time there was no evil, wickedness, or immorality associated with the night. The night was a time to rest, to be rejuvenated and re-energized for the next day. A good night can be a wonderful time to reflect on the guidance, provision, and protection of God throughout that past day.

One of my greatest joys has been watching my children sleep. The more comfortable they were at night, the more I appreciated God's wonderful gifts to me.

The nighttime was never intended to bring fear to mankind. Today will be a good day in your life as you decree it to be.

You can even look forward to bringing glory to God as you knock out some Zs tonight

Proactive Questions—
1. What can I do to get better sleep at night?
2. How can I reflect more of God's love when I wake up in the morning?

Stay on top!

Day 5—Staying in Place: In the Sea, not in a Pocket!

GENESIS 1:20–23 (KJV)
*And God said, Let the waters bring forth abundantly the moving creature that hath life, and fowl that may fly above the earth in the open firmament of heaven. 21 And God created great whales, and every living creature that moveth, which the waters brought forth abundantly, after their kind, and every winged fowl after his kind: and God saw that it was good. 22 And God blessed them, saying, Be fruitful, and multiply, and fill the waters in the seas, and let fowl multiply in the earth. 23 And the evening and the morning were the **fifth** day.*

I am a lover of animals, fish, and birds because I believe God made them for our good and His glory. I am amused when I hear men state that they have just discovered a new species or located a new cavern, etc. I'm sure God is delighted as we discover what He created thousands of years ago. The animals live on the land, the fish stay in the sea, and the birds rule the air. Just the way God planned.

One time when I was living in Portland, Oregon, I was walking to school. I was in the second or third grade. On the way, I found a six-inch-long smelt fish. I thought that was about the coolest thing

I had ever found. I put it in my pocket and went on to school. I showed everyone that day the fish I had found. Well, at the end of the school day, I still had the fish in my pocket.

By the time I finally got home, everybody in the house, maybe even the world, could smell that I was a fish, or had a fish on me. The conclusion I drew was that God intended for fish to live in the sea, not in a little boy's pocket.

Today can be the day you realize that you are right where God wants you to be. You can thank Abba Father.

Proactive Questions—

1. What area or place in my life have I been trying to change even though God has ordained it?
2. Where (either place or position) do you believe God is taking you next?

Stay on top!

Day 6—Here Comes Man

Genesis 1:26, 31 (KJV)

*And God said, Let us make man in our image, after our likeness: and let them have dominion over the fish of the sea, and over the fowl of the air, and over the cattle, and over all the earth, and over every creeping thing that creepeth upon the earth. ... 31 And God saw every thing that he had made, and, behold, it was very good. And the evening and the morning were the **sixth** day.*

Man is like God in that he makes his own decisions. We are free moral agents and can do as we please. We are not given any explanation or details of how God created heavenly creatures, but we are given quite a bit of information on how God created man.

We know that God wanted a being that would voluntarily serve and worship Him.

Today, choose to acknowledge God as Savior and Lord of your life. Man is God's greatest creation, with the greatest capacity to give the greatest praise. Give Him lots of praise today.

Proactive Questions—

1. How can I praise God today like I have never praised Him before?
2. Is there something I haven't thought about for which I should praise God?

Day 7—Almighty God, Creator of Everything

Genesis 2:1–3 (KJV)
*Thus the heavens and the earth were finished, and all the host of them. 2 And on the **seventh** day God ended his work which he had made; and he rested on the seventh day from all his work which he had made. 3 And God blessed the seventh day, and sanctified it: because that in it he had rested from all his work which God created and made.*

As my three children were growing up in Seattle, I would walk by their room many times before going to sleep and observe them sleeping. There is something therapeutic about seeing your family sleeping. While sleeping, it was clear they were totally oblivious to anything around them.

God created our body, soul, and spirit and understands that they need rest on a systematic schedule. The body can rebuild and recoup itself when given the proper rest.

God even rested, not because He was tired or frustrated, but I believe He rested to show us the discipline of stopping to reflect on past actions.

Take this seventh day of devotion and reflect, relax, and rest in the promises of God and His love for you.

Proactive Questions—

1. How can I show God today that I am resting in Him?
2. Who can I encourage today to lighten up, take a break, and relax in God's arms?

Stay on top!

Day 8—Obedience at Any Cost

Genesis 21:4 (KJV) "Eight Days"
*And Abraham circumcised his son Isaac being **eight** days old, as God had commanded him.*

Take it easy, men! Circumcision is easier at eight days than our current ages! Can you imagine Abraham's discomfort in inflicting this pain on the promised son, the one he'd waited on for decades? Abraham, himself had been circumcised at ninety-nine (Gen. 17:24), so he was very well aware of the pain he was about to inflict.

The pain of physical discomfort could not compare to the obligation of being obedient to God. Obedience is better than sacrifice.

2 Kings 22:1 (KJV) "Eight Years"
Josiah was eight years old when he began to reign, and he reigned thirty and one years in Jerusalem.

1 Peter 3:20 (KJV) "Eight Souls"
God waited in the days of Noah, while the ark was preparing, wherein few, that is, eight souls were saved by water.

Proactive **Q**uestions—
1. What was the hardest thing God asked you to obey?
2. How did God bless you after you obeyed?

Stay on top!

Day 9—The Nine: Not Fine

Luke 17:17 (KJV)
*And Jesus answering said, Were there not ten cleansed? But where are the **nine**?*

So many times we find ourselves among the nine lepers who simply didn't take the time to say thanks. Again, as often occurs in the Bible, the players' names are not revealed. What is so much more important than their names is their attitude of gratitude, or lack of it.

The single leper was so thankful and excited that he could think of nothing else but thanking the one who had healed him. I can see him making his way back to Jesus as the other nine quickly went to see the priest.

There was such an additional blessing for the one leper who returned to Jesus. He was able to have personal dialogue with Christ. Christ told him his faith had made him whole. Today is a good day to thank God for all His goodness to you every single day. You will always get the personal attention from Him.

Proactive Statements—

1. God, help me to never overlook the opportunity to say thank you for someone's kindness to me.
2. To say "thank you" does not cost me anything, but it can add lots of value to those serving others.

Stay on top!

Day 10—With My Hands, I Will Praise You!

PSALM 33:2 (KJV)
*Praise the Lord with harp: sing unto him with the psaltery and an instrument of **ten** strings.*

Today I want you to lay both of your instruments (hands) on someone and bless him or her. Every fiber and cell of your body can be used to bless the Lord. As Christ reached out on the Cross with arms stretched wide to mankind, so can we stretch forth our hands and bless God and mankind.

PSALM 47:1 (KJV)
To the chief Musician, 1 A Psalm for the sons of Korah. O clap your hands, all ye people; shout unto God with the voice of triumph.

PSALM 98:8 (KJV)
Let the floods clap their hands: let the hills be joyful together.

Isaiah 55:12 (KJV)

For ye shall go out with joy, and be led forth with peace: the mountains and the hills shall break forth before you into singing, and all the trees of the field shall clap their hands.

Proactive Questions—

1. How can I bless the Lord with my hands today?
2. Can you find a child to bless with your hands today?

Stay on top!

Day 11—And Then There Were Eleven

Matthew 28:16–18 (KJV)
*Then the **eleven** disciples went away into Galilee, into a mountain where Jesus had appointed them. 17 And when they saw him, they **worshipped** him: but **some** doubted. 18 And Jesus came and spake unto them, saying, "All power is given unto me in heaven and in earth."*

Can you imagine the thoughts of the eleven disciples as they counted their number and remembered the demise of Judas? He was the group's treasurer, the one they had fellowshipped with for some three and a half years. Now things were different. Jesus had arisen and been granted all power. What would their next assignment be?

Today is the day I choose to worship and not doubt.

If I want to know the universal sovereignty of Christ, I must know Him myself. I must take time to worship the one whose name I call on and adore.

Philip. 3:10 (KJV)
That I may know him, and the power of his resurrection, and the fellowship of his sufferings, being made conformable unto his death;

I love you, Lord, with all of my heart, and I give my life to you afresh this day. Amen.

Proactive Questions—

1. Have you learned to worship in the midst of doubt?
2. How can I encourage someone that I know is struggling in the midst of his or her situation? Should I call, text, or write? Are there other ways to be encouraging?

__Stay on top!__

Day 12—Spending Quality Time with Jesus

Mark 9:35 (KJV)
*And he sat down, and called the **twelve**, and saith unto them, If any man desire to be first, the same shall be last of all, and servant of all.*

Jesus' disciples had been arguing over who would be the greatest in the kingdom, and He decided to teach them a lesson. Jesus called a child and held him in His arms and let the disciples know that they were to be as humble as a child.

Jesus also let the disciples know that if they wanted to be first, they would have to be last: they would have to be the servants of all. We must first learn what it is to serve before we can be in a position to lead.

Proactive Questions—

1. Have I asked God to remove every bit of selfish ambition that will personally exalt me?
2. Can you think of someone to serve today without looking for anything in return?

Stay on top!

Day 13—In the World, but Not of the World

Joshua 21:19 (KJV)
*All the cities of the children of Aaron, the priests, were **thirteen** cities with their suburbs.*

Today is a good day to remember that you are an alien but not an *undocumented* one. Our identity and lineage can be traced back to the blood of Jesus. Our papers can be found in the pages of the Word of God.

Many would think that the tribe of Levites, descendants from Aaron, would live somewhere by themselves. Not so. By mixing the Levites with the other tribes, they were made to see that the eyes of all Israel were upon them, and therefore it was their concern to walk so that their ministry might not be blamed.

In fact, every tribe had its share of Levites' cities. This was God's way of graciously reminding the Levites to walk in integrity among the people. This plan also helped the people remember their covenant with God.

Saints of God, someone is watching you today and looking up to you. Be your best today.

Proactive Questions—

1. Has God placed you at your address to be His light and salt to your neighbors? They might not read the Bible or go to church.
2. Which of my neighbors is God especially prompting me to pray for today?

Day 14—Loving on God

GENESIS 31:41 (KJV)
*Thus have I been twenty years in thy house; I served thee **fourteen** years for thy two daughters, and six years for thy cattle: and thou hast changed my wages ten times.*

How many times do we give up on the first or second try when doing something that requires physical and mental strength? Serving God requires surrendering everything we have and laying it at the feet of Christ. This journey is not a sprint but rather a marathon.

Jacob's love for Rachel was so strong and ardent that he was willing to work fourteen years for her. Some have never worked seven or fourteen years anywhere, let alone for the love of a woman. To top it off, Jacob's future father-in-law was messing with his money.

Sometimes people mess you over, but just as Jacob was willing to work fourteen years for the woman he loved, we must also be willing to work a lifetime in service for the Master we love. One day, we will spend an eternity with the Master who first loved us.

Proactive Questions—

1. How many years would you be willing to work for someone you love?
2. How can I show God and my spouse that I am willing to work for and with them because I love them?

Stay on top!

Day 15—Sometimes, It's Wall Time

Isaiah 38:1–5 (KJV)

In those days was Hezekiah sick unto death. And Isaiah the prophet the son of Amoz came unto him, and said unto him, Thus saith the Lord, Set thine house in order: for thou shalt die, and not live. 2 Then Hezekiah turned his face toward the wall, and prayed unto the Lord, 3 And said, Remember now, O Lord, I beseech thee, how I have walked before thee in truth and with a perfect heart, and have done that which is good in thy sight. And Hezekiah wept sore.

*4 Then came the word of the Lord to Isaiah, saying, 5 Go, and say to Hezekiah, Thus saith the Lord, the God of David thy father, I have heard thy prayer, I have seen thy tears: behold, I will add unto thy days **fifteen** years.*

Hezekiah had such a relationship with God that he felt comfortable going to God even when he had heard God's decision to call him home. Hezekiah did not ask God for anything. He just reminded God of how he had lived.

Our heavenly father sees our tears and hears our prayers. He has no doubt many times extended us extra time to get our houses (lives) in order.

We serve a loving God that wants to be proven. Hezekiah had the faith and nerves to pray about a decision God had made. It moved the heart and hand of God.

There will be days when you will have to turn to the wall and cry out to God. Be assured, He hears and will answer. Have a great day.

Proactive **Q**uestions—

1. When is the last time you challenged God to prove His Word?
2. How is God testing you now? What do you have to do to prove God?

Stay on top!

Day 16—You Young Whippersnapper!

2 Kings 14:21 (KJV)
*And all the people of Judah took Azariah, which was **sixteen** years old, and made him king instead of his father Amaziah.*

2 Kings 15:2 (KJV)
Sixteen years old was he when he began to reign, and he reigned two and fifty years in Jerusalem. And his mother's name was Jecholiah of Jerusalem.

God didn't care anything about overlooking Amaziah as the next king. Amaziah knew God had chosen his son, Azariah, to be the next king in Jerusalem. I believe the father could rejoice in the fact that God had chosen his son.

2 Chronicles 26:1 (KJV)
*Then all the people of Judah took Uzziah, who was **sixteen** years old, and made him king in the room of his father Amaziah.*

God calls young people into service. Azariah and Uzziah knew God would be with them, and they accepted the challenge.

God blessed their kingships and their names live on as a testimony to God's unlimited mercy and infinite grace.

Proverbs 20:11 (KJV)
Even a child is known by his doings, whether his work be pure, and whether it be right.

Encourage a young person today and bless a little child.

Proactive Questions—

1. Name a relative that would love to hear from you today.
2. What could you say to encourage that relative on life's journey?

Stay on top!

Day 17—When Bad Things Happen to Good People

Genesis 37:2 (GW)
*This is the account of Jacob and his descendants. Joseph was a **seventeen-year-old** young man. He took care of the flocks with the sons of Bilhah and Zilpah, his father's wives. Joseph told his father about the bad things his brothers were doing.*

Joseph was a good lad, but he was a little naïve at times. God never pointed out to Joseph all the dangers and set-backs he would have to endure. Because Joseph endured and keep the right attitude, in time God exalted him.

Many times, we just don't understand what is happening when we have done good things. That is a good time to thank God for what He is up to. We don't have to always see what God is doing to know that He is working for us.

Despite being sold by his brothers and spending two years in prison, Joseph persevered and was able to save his own family. The palace was always there. God turned things around in Joseph's favor.

Have a wonderful day today. You are on your way to the palace.

Proactive Questions—
1. Is there something happening in your life right now that you are trusting God for victory?
2. How can you help others when your own life feels like a prison?

Stay on top!

Day 18—Straighten Up and Fly Right

LUKE 13:11; 16 (KJV)
*And, behold, there was a woman which had a spirit of infirmity **eighteen** years, and was bowed together, and could in no wise lift up herself... 16 And ought not this woman, being a daughter of Abraham, whom Satan hath bound, lo, these eighteen years, be loosed from this bond on the Sabbath day?*

As a young man growing up, I would often hear someone tell another person to straighten up and fly right. This meant that the person in question needed to get the right attitude and move forward.

Can you imagine how this lady felt when Christ healed her? For eighteen years she had been bent over. She was bound by a spirit of infirmity. I'm sure she had a grateful heart.

Remember that God wants the best for His children, no matter how long you may have been bound by Satan. God wants you free!

Call on Him today, and he will do great and mighty things in your life (Jer. 33:3).

Proactive Questions—

1. Have you ever thought of your infirmities or strong temptations as being controlled by a spirit?
2. What have you found to be the best way to fight an ungodly spirit?

Stay on top!

Day 19—You Are the Declared Winner!

2 SAMUEL 2:30–31 (KJV)
*And Joab returned from following Abner: and when he had gathered all the people together, there lacked of David's servants **nineteen** men and Asahel. But the servants of David had smitten of Benjamin, and of Abner's men, so that three hundred and threescore men died.*

This was a civil war between God's people. It really should have never taken place. We must learn to love our brothers and sisters. If we look hard enough, we can find something good in everyone. Praise God for His goodness to man. His love endureth forever.

Remember, today you can be a casualty, or you can be the winner. It is your choice. The Bible says we are the conquerors in Christ Jesus. Stay in the Word and make sure the Word is in you.

Proactive Questions-
1. What is the Scripture that you use most to help bring victory in the midst of your trial?
2. How can you help a friend or family member who is way out of harmony with the rest of the family?

Stay on top!

Day 20—Counting the Cost

Luke 14:31 (KJV)
*Or what king, going to make war against another king, sitteth not down first, and consulteth whether he be able with ten thousand to meet him that cometh against him with **twenty** thousand?*

God instructs us to count the cost in our endeavor to live a godly life. Make no mistake; we are in a war, a war for the control of our minds. Satan wants to make us think that we don't have the goods to fight and win, but we do.

Today we can start our worship and praise with the fruit of our lips. God just loves to hear us call on Him. It helps us to know where all of our help comes from.

David said:

Give ear to my words, O Lord, consider my meditation. Hearken unto the voice of my cry, my King, and my God: for unto thee will I pray. My voice shalt thou hear in the morning, O Lord; in the morning will I direct my prayer unto thee, and will look up. (Psalm 5:3)

Count the cost each morning as you seek God. You will definitely begin with a greater resolve.

Proactive Questions—

1. Do you have someone in your life who is a good counter? Someone who tells it to you straight?
2. What do you do when the count is all wrong and no one is there to help you?

Stay on top!

Day 21—The Answer Is Coming

Daniel 10:13
*But the prince of the kingdom of Persia withstood me **one and twenty days**: but, lo, Michael, one of the chief princes, came to help me; and I remained there with the kings of Persia.*

Daniel had prayed twenty-one days before he heard from God. Many times we give up too soon and throw in the towel. You must remember that God hears you the very first time you call His name.

Be assured there is war in the heavens. We ultimately win in the end, because God is greater than anything the Devil or man can conjure up. Whatever tries to hold you back from doing all God has required will fall now or in the proverbial twenty-one days.

Keep praying, toiling, praying, toiling on; there soon will come a brighter day; keep praying, toiling on.

These particular words ring in my mind. I remember singing them many times in church as I was growing up. I now understand those words much better. Prayer for me has become a way of life. The answer is on its way.

Proactive Questions—

1. Write down the particular thing you are trusting God for. Do you believe that God has heard you and has already dispatched an angel to carry out His desires?
2. What is the last prayer you remember God answering?

Stay on top!

Day 22—Fear Not!

JUDGES 7:3 (GW)
*Announce to the troops, "Whoever is scared or frightened should leave Mount Gilead and go back home." So **22,000** men went back home, and 10,000 were left.*

Gideon was instructed by God to reduce the size of his army. He started with thirty-two thousand, and after using God's subtraction instruction, his army was reduced to just three hundred.

God wanted Gideon to know that he was not going to win this battle by his numbers and weaponry. They were going to depend on the power and authority of God Almighty. The first to be removed from Gideon's army were those who were afraid to fight or die.

Every Christian must have something in his or her spirit that is worth dying for. Then and only then are you ready to really live for what you believe. God can take a little and work miracles. Two fish and five small loaves of bread fed five thousand men plus their families.

Today is a great time to declare your dependence on God to fight your battles in every area of your life. You will come out the winner every time.

Proactive Questions—
1. Why is having a smaller group of cohesive men better than an army of scared individuals?
2. When was the last time you were scared of something? And what did you do?

Stay on top!

Day 23—Each Day Makes a Difference

1 Corinthians 10:8–9 (KJV)
*Neither let us commit fornication, as some of them committed, and fell in one day **three and twenty thousand**. Neither let us tempt Christ, as some of them also tempted, and were destroyed of serpents.*

As you start your day, you must be aware that Satan didn't sleep last night. He is planning your demise today. But thank God we are not afraid of his plans or weapons (Is. 54:17).

However, it is a sobering thought that twenty-three thousand of God's chosen people would backslide in one day by committing immoral acts of the flesh. This happened even after they witnessed the parting of the Red Sea and ate the food that fell from heaven. All that was not enough to keep them from sinning.

Let's determine to stay focused and prayed up as we put on our armor before going out the door. Make sure you stop by your prayer closet before you leave. We are more than conquerors, the Bible says (Rom. 8:37).

Proactive Questions—
1. Can you name a few things in your life that you could eventually take for granted?
2. What is the best way to keep humble before the Lord?

Stay on top!

Day 24—The Mind of Worship

Rev. 11:16–18 (KJV)
*And the **four and twenty elders**, which sat before God on their seats, fell upon their faces, and worshipped God, Saying, We give thee thanks, O Lord God Almighty, which art, and wast, and art to come; because thou hast taken to thee thy great power, and hast reigned.*

I look forward to the day we join with the twenty-four elders, who are symbolic of the twelve tribes of Israel and the twelve Apostles. In fact, why not join with them right now and worship God in your own way? God has been so good to us throughout the years; He deserves all of our praise and worship.

I can only imagine how Satan hates it when we break out in worship, let alone how much he must hate the Christian who has learned to live in a mindset and attitude of worship.

When we all get to heaven, all of creation in heaven, earth, and under the earth will join together in a mighty thunderous spontaneous *worship!* Awesome!

Proactive Questions—

1. Where is the most unusual place that you felt led to worship God?

2. One day when Christ returns, the Bible says we will have a new body. How will this enhance your worship to God?

Stay on top!

Day 25—Just Do the Right Thing

1 Kings 22:41–43 (KJV)
And Jehoshaphat the son of Asa began to reign over Judah in the fourth year of Ahab king of Israel.

*42 Jehoshaphat was thirty and five years old when he began to reign; and he reigned **twenty and five years** in Jerusalem. And his mother's name was Azubah the daughter of Shilhi.*

43 And he walked in all the ways of Asa his father; he turned not aside from it, doing that which was right in the eyes of the LORD …

If you have read your Bible at all, especially the Old Testament, it does not take long to see that everyone that became a king was not always good. The father could be a good king and the son a wicked one, or vice versa.

Jehoshaphat determined to be an obedient and faithful king. For twenty-five years he did the right thing.

We may never reach a position of ruling over thousands and thousands of people, but God has entrusted some people to your sphere of influence. Today, someone will be observing you. That person may even have an unrealistic expectation of you. You may think it is unfair, and yet so it is.

As this morning dawns, ask God to empower you afresh with the precious Holy Spirit. If God be for you, who or what can stand against you? No one knows how much time he or she has left on earth, but one thing we do control is our determination and resolve to do the right thing. This is the day!

Proactive Questions—

1. Can you name a couple of things that you intend to praise God for, no matter what?
2. What have you learned about just doing the right thing that you could pass on to a newer Christian?

Stay on top!

Day 26—You Are Making a Difference

1 CHRONICLES 7:39–40 (KJV)

And the sons of Ulla; Arah, and Haniel, and Rezia. ⁴⁰ All these were the children of Asher, heads of their father's house, choice and mighty men of valour, chief of the princes. And the number throughout the genealogy of them that were apt to the war and to battle was **twenty and six thousand** *men.*

Here we have four mighty men who had earned the right to be the head of their fathers' houses. They were battle-tried and tested and probably had the scars to prove it. They were the cream of the crop, chief among the princes.

These men had so conducted themselves that they inspired the men in their families to prepare themselves for war. In fact, there was such devotion and vigor that twenty-six thousand men signed up to serve under these four mighty sons.

You are making a difference in your family, school, community, and church. Others will follow in your steps. Be real; be genuine; be the real deal. You will inspire others to take up the battle and stand in the gap. Notice Isaiah:

Also I heard the voice of the Lord, saying, Whom shall I send, and who will go for us? Then said I, Here am I; send me. (Isaiah 6:8 KJV)

You lead the right way, and you will find many that will be inspired by your passion and desire for God. Not just in this generation, but also in the generations that follow.

Proactive Questions—

1. Can you name a couple of people who have made a great impression on your life because of their lives in God?
2. What are a couple of things you believe God will make happen during your lifetime?

Stay on top!

Day 27—Destined for Greatness

Genesis 23:1 (KJV)
*And Sarah was an **hundred and seven and twenty years** old: these were the years of the life of Sarah.*

I believe that every woman of God is destined for greatness in her own way. The God I serve is not at all limited by our petite thinking. You are ultimately defined by your spiritual heritage and not your natural parents or current situation.

As far as we know, Sarah had only one child. This one child was the child of promise: Isaac. First of all, Sarah had to endure verbal abuse from other people, especially other women that didn't have an inkling or bit of insight into the power and promise of God for her life.

If Abraham is the father of the Jewish nation, then we must deduct that Sarah was the mother of the Jewish nation. She was obviously a fine-looking lady, judging by Abraham's attempt to deceive others into believing she was his sister on a couple of occasions. By the way, Abraham got in trouble for doing that.

Sarah laughed at the thought of having a baby at such an old age. After all, she was an old lady, way past childbearing age. God worked a miracle through her. God is still working miracles today in the hearts and souls of people that yield themselves to Him.

Today may be the start of the one thing in you that the world will read and rejoice about years and years from now. Just be open to the hand of God.

Proactive Questions—

1. Do you believe that God is still working miracles in this mean and wicked world? What have you noticed about God's activity in the world?
2. How has God shown you to love your enemy? If you have none, then how do you love someone who seems unlovable?

Stay on top!

Day 28—The Gift of Singing

Ezra 2:1; 41 (KJV)
Now these are the children of the province that went up out of the captivity, of those which had been carried away, whom Nebuchadnezzar the king of Babylon had carried away unto Babylon, and came again unto Jerusalem and Judah, every one unto his city; [41] *The singers: the children of Asaph, an* **hundred twenty and eight.**

When Joseph's family came to Egypt to escape the famine, no one could have imagined that they would be there seventy years. Joseph gave instruction to take his body with them when they made their exodus.

God didn't forget about the singers: the children of Asaph. Psalm 87:7 states that the singers will be there in heaven. I just know God loves good singing. For the rest of us, we can make a joyful noise.

If God has given you the talent of singing, use it or lose it. It was given to you to help build the kingdom of God, one soul at a time.

What a wonderful day to re-dedicate the talent or gift God has given you. Everything we have that is good and perfect comes from the father above. Bless the Lord, oh my soul, and all that is within me.

Proactive Questions—

1. What is the talent you think God has given you?

2. Do you know someone you could call today and encourage to start using a singing gift for the Creator who gave it to him or her? What would you say to him or her?

Stay on top!

Day 29—The Gift from Mother

2 Chronicles 29:1–2 (KJV)
*Hezekiah began to reign when he was five and twenty years old, and he reigned **nine and twenty years** in Jerusalem. And his mother's name was Abijah, the daughter of Zechariah. And he did that which was right in the sight of the Lord, according to all that David his father had done.*

I seldom, if ever, hear big, burly, rough-looking football players giving any hellos or waves to their fathers. It is always to mothers. There is something special and unique about a mother's love and influence on her children. I'm sure it wasn't any different for Hezekiah. I believe he had a godly mother.

Please notice the title for this devotion does not say the gift *of* mother, but rather the gift *from* mother. A mother in herself is not necessarily a good thing to her child. I'm sure we have heard about the terrible things a biological mother can do to her children.

The gifts *from* a good mother are the values, training, discipline, and, most of all, godly life that is daily lived before her children. This is something that cannot be valued monetarily.

I'm sure Hezekiah's mother, Abijah, had a lot to do with this young man serving faithfully for twenty-nine years as Jerusalem's king. Thank God for a mother's gift, which can impact her children and their children. In your prayers today, pray for all the mothers and especially for the single mothers that struggle to serve as both parents. God bless you.

Proactive Questions—

1. What is the one thing that you received from your mother, or the person you call Mother, that you will always cherish?
2. What would you say to the single mother today who is struggling and trying to make ends meet?

Stay on top!

Day 30—Choose Life

> LUKE 3:23 (KJV)
> *And Jesus himself began to be about **thirty** years of age, being (as was supposed) the son of Joseph, which was the son of Heli...*

> MATTHEW 27:3 (KJV)
> *Then Judas, which had betrayed him, when he saw that he was condemned, repented himself, and brought again the **thirty** pieces of silver to the chief priests and elders...*

We have a young man named Jesus who is about to embark on the greatest journey any man could make. He has been sent by God Himself to be the final, perfect sacrifice. After Christ, there would be no other sacrifice necessary. Jesus had spent thirty earthly years waiting to finish His purpose on earth.

Somewhere in the temple, Judas had made a negotiation. The cost of this potential life-ending deal was the sum of thirty pieces of silver. Isn't that the same number our Lord and Savior chose to wait for to begin His ministry? Thirty years begins Christ ministry; the other sum of thirty pieces betrays Christ ministry.

Every day, we have to choose between life and death. The choices come in many different forms and shapes. Sometimes we can recover from wrong choices and bad decisions. Other times, we can't. Thank God you have another wonderful day in front of you to be a blessing to someone who is about to give up. Choose life.

Proactive Questions—

1. Can you surmise why society has taken the sanctity of life so casually?
2. What do you say to a young, pregnant woman who is considering terminating her pregnancy?

Stay on top!

Day 31—A Vessel of Honor

2 KINGS 22:1–2 (KJV)
Josiah was eight years old when he began to reign, and he reigned **thirty and one years** *in Jerusalem. And his mother's name was Jedidah, the daughter of Adaiah of Boscath. ² And he did that which was right in the sight of the Lord, and walked in all the way of David his father, and turned not aside to the right hand or to the left.*

Yes, you read right. Josiah was just eight years old when he began a thirty-one-year reign as king in Jerusalem. As I look at this last devotional Scripture for the last day of this month, I stand in wonder and amazement at the hand, heart, and face of God.

If God could use an eight-year-old boy and make him king, then he could use anyone that would stay on the potter's wheel and let Him mold him or her into the vessel He ordained them to be before the world began. Praise God!

Our souls cry out for God in a most desperate way. We have the DNA of the creator of the universe flowing in our natural and spiritual veins. By the way they are still discovering more galaxies and star systems. There are no new creations; they have always been there.

I'm sure God is amused by our stumbling onto some unknown cavern or deep ocean sea life that produces its own light in a pitch-black atmosphere. There is so much pressure per square inch at that depth, no man and very few devices we have made can live or operate in such an environment.

Miles below the surface, in a cold and dark world, and yet—what is that? A jellyfish that one can see through. And it can survive and thrive down there, with its very own defense system.

What a mighty God we serve!

Do we need more Josiahs or Hezekiahs? I say no! What we need is more of God and less of us. The name of the vessel is not as important as the use of the vessel. I'm willing to be used by God to the max. How about you?

This is the day ... *Stay on top!*

Proactive Questions—

1. How can you be more effective in telling the story of the Savior who died for our sins?
2. Can you be more effective in showing the love of God to the lost and dying?

TWENTY-ONE-DAY FAST

Inspirations
Pastor Otis F. Brown Jr.

**In honor and memory of
Drs. Otis and Johnnie Mae Brown**

Day 1

Daniel 9:3 (KJV)
And I set my face unto the Lord God, to seek by prayer and supplications, with fasting, and sackcloth, and ashes:

As you began this twenty-one-day fast today, let God know what you expect Him to do for you and what you will do for Him. Confess and decree the Word of God. Speak faith-filled words. It is the Word of God that will move the hand of God.

I pray that the God of the universe becomes so intimate and present with and in you that these twenty-one days draw you into the Holy of Holies and serve as a genesis of consistent and purposeful self-discipline. You can make it if you try!

Day 2

Daniel 9:4 (GW)
I prayed to the Lord my God. I confessed and said, "Lord, you are great and deserve respect as the only God. You keep your promise and show mercy to those who love you and obey your commandments."

On this second day of the fast, stay focused on your purpose and goal. Physically, the hardest part of the fast will be the first two or three days. After that, you will settle into a pattern and will be able to focus even more on the spiritual.

Day 3

One group of middle-class believers in a church in the UK decided to live on the minimum wage. Their goal was to identify with those who live on little, to learn the joy of giving, to invite God to change their attitudes toward money, and to challenge others in their church to do the same. For their study, they chose Isaiah, chapter 58.

Afterward, one of the leaders said that they had learned an important lesson. Living on less "makes you realize just how much you really can give away."

Give yourself to God afresh today. He will anoint and inspire you to walk in the power of God in places you never thought possible.

Day 4

Isaiah 58:6 (KJV)
Is not this the fast that I have chosen? to loose the bands of wickedness, to undo the heavy burdens, and to let the oppressed go free, and that ye break every yoke?

We see from this verse that fasting should always have a purpose and goal. The power of fasting can break the power of wickedness and lift heavy burdens and set the captives free. Keep going, my brothers and sisters.

Day 5

James 4:8 (KJV)
Draw nigh to God, and he will draw nigh to you. Cleanse your hands, ye sinners; and purify your hearts, ye double minded.

I'm sure by now you feel yourself drawing closer to God. As you do so, you will clearly see the things God wants you to set aside, such as an attitude God wants you to change, or a mind-set . Choose the mind of Christ today (Phil. 2:5). Be blessed!

Day 6

Hey, keep up the good work!

Real and effective fasting by a Christian is not simply fasting from food, but also fasting from eloquence, from impressive diction, and from everything else that might hinder the witness of God in your life.

Be ready for distractions. God has given you a spirit of power and love; nothing can hurt you. Go forth!

Day 7

Well, today marks the first third of the journey through this fast. If you have made it this far, you are beginning to hear God much more clearly. The more disciplined you are, the more God will use you. The song "All the way" says "I'm going all the way with the Lord."

Day 8

ECCLESIASTES 11:1 (KJV)
Cast thy bread upon the waters: for thou shalt find it after many days.

You should now have established a rhythm in your fast. You should also be able to recognize old Slew foot and his old tricks. He will never give up trying to get you back on his side. He is a loser.

The successful things you do today will create your future tomorrow. Keep moseying on down the track; God is with you.

Day 9

GALATIANS 6:9 (KJV)
And let us not be weary in well doing: for in due season we shall reap, if we faint not.

Focus today on doing things well. You will sometimes be tired or irritated; that's a part of life. Remember harvest time is coming. This season will end and a new season will begin. Don't faint!

Day 10

II Samuel 12:16
David therefore besought God for the child; and David fasted, and went in, and lay all night upon the earth.

David understood what it was to go to God with your entire, soul, mind, and spirit. Many times, David would seek God's direction before going into battle.

Fasting is one of the quickest ways to bring flesh into subjection. You have counted the cost and are on your journey through life. I pray this will be a good day.

Day 11

Ezra 8:21 (GW)
Then I announced a fast there at the Ahava River so that we might humble ourselves in the presence of our God to ask him for a safe journey for ourselves, for our little ones, and for all our goods.

Humble yourself today and ask God for direction. Not just for you but also for those God has entrusted in your care. Remember, you are not trying to convince God to bless you or do something for you that is already spoken or implied in His Word. We are simply taking hold of God's willingness to fulfill His Word.

Keep going with your fast; you are right on target!

Day 12

JOEL 1:14 (GW)
*Schedule a time to **fast**! Call for an assembly! Gather the leaders and everyone who lives in the land. Bring them to the temple of the Lord your God, and cry to the Lord for help.*

We are fasting this month not just because it has become a tradition, but also to call on God for direction, to humble ourselves and seek His forgiveness.

Then we can rise and go forth this year with the complete assurance that God is going before us. This will be an awesome time. We declare and decree it. *You can make it!*

Day 13

JOEL 2:12–13
*Therefore also now, saith the Lord, turn ye even to me with all your heart, and with **fasting**, and with weeping, and with mourning: And rend your heart, and not your garments, and turn unto the Lord your God: for he is gracious and merciful, slow to anger, and of great kindness ...*

Run to God when you blow it. Don't run from Him. God knows we are but flesh and bone. That is why He sent Jesus to die in your place. God simply wants a broken and contrite heart. He can work with that. Your fasting will draw you closer to God today. Have a victorious day!

Day 14

MATTHEW 6:16–18 (KJV)
*Moreover when ye **fast**, be not, as the hypocrites, of a sad countenance: for they disfigure their faces, that they may appear unto men to fast. Verily I say unto you, they have their reward.*

17 But thou, when thou fastest, anoint thine head, and wash thy face; 18 That thou appear not unto men to fast, but unto thy Father which is in secret: and thy Father, which seeth in secret, shall reward thee openly.

We are not fasting to impress anyone. We are fasting to bring our flesh into subjection to the Spirit of the living God.

You can be sure people will tempt you by offering you food and other temptations that will test your discipline. Be of good cheer; that only means it's working. You are getting closer to God. You hear Him quicker and more plainly than before. It can only get better as you hang in there. God is up to something good for you (Jer. 29:11).

Day 15

ACTS 14:23 (KJV)
*And when they had ordained them elders in every church, and had prayed with **fasting**, they commended them to the Lord, on whom they believed.*

There are some things in life we should never do until we have prayed and fasted before God. The ordination of an individual, the starting of a ministry, the dedication of a child, and any other major event in our lives should be bathed with prayer and fasting.

After we have prayed and fasted, we should find rest in our spirit as we commend or give it to the Lord. We are limited in our abilities to change people and make them do right, but we can set the atmosphere and stage for God to move in His own sovereign way. His thoughts and ways are far better and higher than ours (see Is. 55:8–9).

Day 16

Acts 10:30 (KJV)
*And Cornelius said, Four days ago I was **fasting** until this hour; and at the ninth hour I prayed in my house, and, behold, a man stood before me in bright clothing,*

Like Cornelius, the head of the first gentile Christian family, you just might be the first person in your family to receive the Holy Spirit.

Today give yourself totally, 100 percent, to God. This could start a spiritual avalanche, a Holy Ghost hurricane that sweeps through your family, church, and community. I dare you to give yourself to God, without any conditions attached

Jesus spoke this words in Luke 22:42 (KJV)[42] Saying, Father, if thou be willing, remove this cup from me: nevertheless not my will, but thine, be done.

It's just a few more days till the fast ends. Thank God for every temptation and your victory over Satan, who desperately wants to abort your spiritual formation. You are blessed!

Day 17

Luke 2:36–37 (KJV)
*And there was one Anna, a prophetess, the daughter of Phanuel, of the tribe of Aser: she was of a great age, and had lived with an husband seven years from her virginity; [37] And she was a widow of about fourscore and four years, which departed not from the temple, but served God with **fastings** and prayers night and day.*

Anna, a widow, lived at the church for decades. She apparently had decided not to remarry, but to give herself to God and His work. She was full of the Holy Spirit and blessed Joseph and Mary when they came to the temple with baby Jesus.

Anna was always ready to fast and pray. I believed if someone expressed a sincere need or problem, she was ready to go in prayer to God. She knew that God is tuned to those who offer themselves in this manner.

Today, think of someone else going through a problem and send up a portion of your fasting and prayer for him or her. Today is a good day to love on God.

Day 18

ESTHER 4:16 (KJV)
*Go, gather together all the Jews that are present in Shushan, and **fast** ye for me, and neither eat nor drink three days, night or day: I also and my maidens will fast likewise; and so will I go in unto the king, which is not according to the law: and if I perish, I perish.*

Queen Esther had been divinely selected to be the instrument of God to save the Jewish people.

What I like about Esther is that she realized the power of a corporate fast. She was not trusting in her position or her beauty. She knew the power of a people that have joined together to seek the help of almighty God.

This year, our church can reach pinnacles never attainable in a divided church. Together we stand, divided we collapse on ourselves. I choose unity and life.

In your devotion today, especially remember your church family and leaders.

Day 19

> ACTS 14:23 (GW)
> *They had the disciples in each church choose spiritual leaders, and with prayer and **fasting** they entrusted the leaders to the Lord in whom they believed.*

What would happen if families, churches, communities, and even the governments had a time of prayer and fasting before selections, elections, and appointments? What kind of world would we have?

The disciples understood that they could not be everywhere in the region. Some of them had been with and traveled with Jesus. They simply had to do the best they could to help train and equip men to serve as the elders and leaders in the newly formed churches.

They did the best thing they could do after doing their part: to pray and fast and then place the leaders in the hands of God.

You are coming to the end of the fast, and by now you might be experiencing greater insight into how much God loves to interact with His creation. God loves to communicate with us. Keep trusting God to deal with the situations at hand. We can take a lesson from the disciples.

Day 19

> ACTS 14:23 (GW)
> *They had the disciples in each church choose spiritual leaders, and with prayer and **fasting** they entrusted the leaders to the Lord in whom they believed.*

What would happen if families, churches, communities, and even the governments had a time of prayer and fasting before selections, elections, and appointments? What kind of world would we have?

The disciples understood that they could not be everywhere in the region. Some of them had been with and traveled with Jesus. They simply had to do the best they could to help train and equip men to serve as the elders and leaders in the newly formed churches.

They did the best thing they could do after doing their part: to pray and fast and then place the leaders in the hands of God.

You are coming to the end of the fast, and by now you might be experiencing greater insight into how much God loves to interact with His creation. God loves to communicate with us. Keep trusting God to deal with the situations at hand. We can take a lesson from the disciples.

Day 20

DEUTERONOMY 9:9 (GW)
When I went up on the mountain to get the stone tablets, the tablets of the promise that the Lord made to you, I stayed on the mountain forty days and forty nights without food or water.

God has servants that have the heart of God; they are willing to give of themselves, their possessions, their future, and even their lives for the salvation and good of the people God has entrusted to them. You simply must have the heart of a faithful shepherd, who is willing to stand between the sheep and danger.

Jesus did that for us, and His pastors must be willing to do the same. Forty days without food or water seems like an impossible feat. Moses had to be caught up in the Spirit. He entered a realm where natural food and water became a type of distraction.

You have done well on this fast, I trust, with one more day left. All church leaders should resolve to be leaders who are willing to be alone with God.

Being alone with God will expose every weakness you have and even ones you didn't know you had. But it is worth it. This great work is not about us, but rather about advancing the kingdom of God by winning one soul at a time.

Day 21

1 Kings 19:7–8 (GW)
The angel of the Lord came back and woke him up again. The angel said, "Get up and eat, or your journey will be too much for you."

8 He got up, ate, and drank. Strengthened by that food, he traveled for forty days and nights until he came to Horeb, the mountain of God.

Praise God, you made it: twenty-one days of fasting. As God sent the angel to tell Elijah to get up and eat naturally, God is saying the same thing to us spiritually. You must fortify yourselves with the Word.

You simply cannot and will not be able to survive the onslaught of the enemies' fiery darts unless you engulf yourself in the living Word.

John 1:14 (KJV)
And the Word was made flesh, and dwelt among us, (and we beheld his glory, the glory as of the only begotten of the Father,) full of grace and truth.

JOHN 14:6 (KJV)
Jesus saith unto him, I am the way, the truth, and the life: no man cometh unto the Father, but by me.

God bless and keep you, and may you always be chasing after God.

We are the winners!

About the Author

Pastor Otis Brown Jr. has been described as a humble man, believing the way up is down on your knees. Pastor Brown is the son of Pastor Brown Sr., who served fifty years in ministry. Otis Jr. has two children and several grandchildren.

Otis worked in the construction industry for thirty-one years. During the last eight years of his construction career, he also worked as a pastor.

Pastor Brown lost his first wife of twenty-eight years and his oldest daughter within a year and a half. This experience has uniquely qualified Otis, who is an eternal optimist, to write this devotional.

Pastor Brown moved to Tucson, Arizona in 1996 and is now married to Lendor Brown. He earned a degree in theological studies. He is currently the pastor of Siloam Freewill Church of the Christian and Missionary Alliance.

CPSIA information can be obtained
at www.ICGtesting.com
Printed in the USA
FSOW01n1506250615
8260FS